Print information available on the last page

Rev. date: 10/07/2016

To order additional copies of this book, contact:
Xlibris
1-888-795-4274
www.Xlibris.com
Orders@Xlibris.com

Little Santos was excited about graduation. He realized he had just completed 14 years of school beginning in pre-kinder and finally coming to the end of his 12th grade year. Passing from elementary to junior high was one stepping stone. Three years of junior high then high school was yet another. Leaving high school was an even bigger and more important step! He began to think about all the possibilities. What would Little Santos do now? What would he become?

After graduation day, Little Santos knew he had to try and find a job. It wasn't going to be easy. He quickly realized his learning disability was interfering with his ability to get through a job application process. One morning, while he was eating breakfast and reading the newspaper, he came across an announcement that his city was seeking applicants for the fire department. Little Santos thought to himself, "I want to try this." "I want to be a firefighter!"

That afternoon, he remembered one of his friends had completed the fire academy a few years ago. Little Santos wanted to find out more information about becoming a firefighter so he went to visit his friend, Joshua. His friend said, "You have to be strong and courageous to be a firefighter!" Little Santos felt discouraged. He thought he was too small to be a firefighter.

The next morning Little Santos asked himself, "What do I have to lose?" He then got the courage to walk straight to city hall to ask for a firefighter application. He filled out the application and turned it in that same day. He was scheduled to take the entrance exam.

When the time came to take the exam, all he could do was try his best, and he did.

Little Santos took a big breath as he looked at the list of all the people that took the test that day. He searched and searched for his score. The scores were listed in order from highest to lowest. He was having a little trouble finding his score so he asked the receptionist for help. To his amazement, his score was at the top of the list. Out of one hundred people that took the test that day, he was number five with a score of 97. Little Santos was so excited and he jumped for joy. He couldn't wait to start the fireman's academy.

The first day of the fire academy was very overwhelming for Little Santos. He had struggled in school his whole life, but he wanted to prove to himself that he could do it. He wasn't going to stop trying. He wasn't going to give up. During training class the instructor said, "If you fail 3 tests, you're out of here!" Little Santos thought to himself, "The academy is seven months long and we have to take three test a week... Oh boy...This was not going to be easy."

Well, it was time for the first test. All Little Santos kept thinking over and over again was what the instructor said on the first day of the academy. He knew he had to pass. He turned in his test and waited for the results. The instructor began passing out the test. Little Santos held his breath as he opened the test. He failed the test. Little Santos thought, "How am I going to make it?"

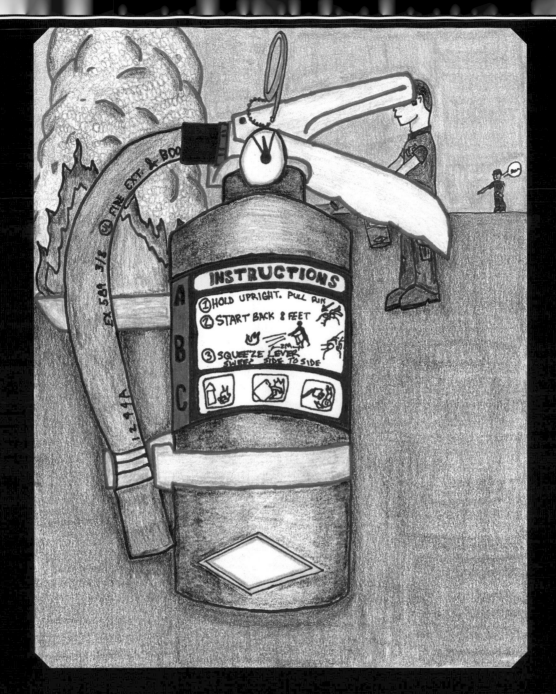

Little Santos put his pride aside and got up every morning to report to class. Little Santos began learning new things. He learned about fire extinguishers. It didn't sound like fun at first, but Little Santos thought, "Its good stuff to know." **Step 1**...Pull the pin. **Step 2**...Aim at what you're going to put out. **Step 3**...Squeeze the trigger to release the agent. **Step 4**... Sweep the nozzle side to side. The instructor would shout, ***"Sweep! Sweep!"***

The following week, Little Santos learned about vehicle stability and hydraulic tools. He had an opportunity to use a controlling device for supported strong bags. It was so cool to move a very big vehicle with such a small button.

Little Santos didn't want to fail another test, so he visited a teacher he knew could help him. Studying was not something he knew how to do well, but he knew what it was going to take to be a firefighter.

Learning how to use a fire hose was exciting for Little Santos. He watched as the instructor turned on the pump to high pressure. As the water traveled through the hose, it started to go crazy. Up and down and all around. Little Santos was not afraid, he was having fun getting all wet and muddy. He was able to control the hose with no problems. Everybody cheered.

Some people are afraid of heights, but not Little Santos. He's not afraid to go up ladders, or climb buildings. He knows it's important for firefighters to be strong enough to do these things in order to save lives. Whenever you feel scared, just take a deep breath to relax. If Little Santos can do it, you can too.

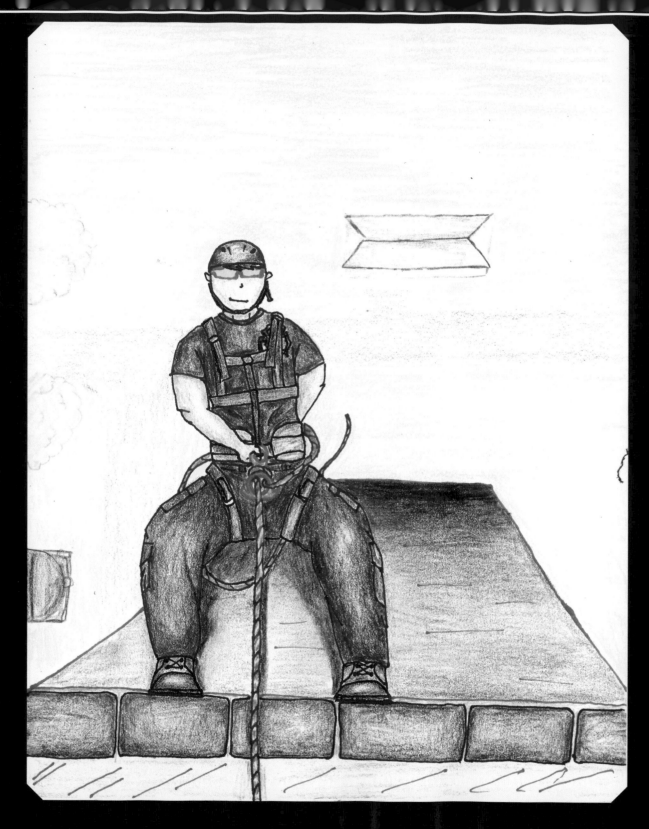

Repelling off a four-story building was not easy for Little Santos. He had never done this before. But Little Santos didn't let that stop him from trying something new. Anything is possible as long as you try your best.

Learning about hazardous material was awesome. Little Santos had to wear protective clothing called a Hazmat suit. All the suits were too big for Little Santos, but that didn't stop him from showing off his skills just like everyone else. Nothing was going to stop him from being a firefighter.

Little Santos liked the SCBA class. SCBA stands for self-contained breathing apparatus. The instructor was nice and explained everything so Little Santos could understand. He felt like he was finally learning. The instructor encouraged Little Santos and kept pushing him to be better.

Little Santos took his second test and failed again. This time with a 69. He couldn't believe he failed the test by only one point. He didn't want to be let go from the fire academy. He didn't want to disappoint his parents. The thought of failing again made him angry, but he knew he had to try even harder. He wasn't going to give up on his dream of becoming a firefighter.

The fire chief stopped to talk to Little Santos. He didn't know what he was going to tell him. He was scared. Little Santos began to ask himself, "Is he going to fire me?" "Is he going to send me home?" The fire chief told Little Santos, "If you fail one more test, I will have to send you home, but don't give up because we believe in you!" Even though the chief was tough on all the firemen, he motivated Little Santos to do even better.

The skills being taught were getting harder and harder for Little Santos. It was very demanding work for his little body. He was smaller than all the other men, so be began to doubt his physical abilities. It came time to use the *Jaws of Life*. To the surprise of all watching, including the instructor, it was easy for Little Santos. He pulled that car apart with ease. Little Santos kept thinking..."I will never quit!"..."I will never give up!"

Live fire training is something all firefighters look forward to. Little Santos was so excited to begin this part of the training, he was the first one to grab the nozzle. Little Santos wanted to show his fellow classmates that he was ready.

The big day finally arrived. Little Santos was going to take the state exam. The test was timed, so he was nervous. He knew he couldn't read as fast as his classmates. He knew odds were against him, but he was determined to become a fireman. He took his time and read everything very carefully. He answered all the questions and turned in his final exam.

When the results of the test were announced, he couldn't believe his ears. The instructor called out his name and presented him with the fireman badge. He did it! Little Santos was a fireman. His faith, hard work, and dedication paid off.

Little Santos was hired and wore his uniform with pride. He was ready for his first emergency call and his first fire truck ride.

Printed in the United States
By Bookmasters